Designer Scrapbooks
The Red Hat Society Way

Designer Scrapbooks

The Red Hat Society Way

By Ruby RedHat

Foreword by Exalted Queen Mother Sue Ellen Cooper

Sterling Publishing Co., Inc. New York

A Sterling/Chapelle Book

Chapelle, Ltd., Inc., P.O. Box 9252, Ogden, UT 84409
(801) 621-2777 • (801) 621-2788 Fax
e-mail: chapelle@chapelleltd.com
Web site: www.chapelleltd.com

A Red Lips 4 Courage book
Red Lips 4 Courage Communications, Inc.
8502 E. Chapman Ave., 303
Orange, CA 92869
Web site: www.redlips4courage.com

Space would not permit the inclusion of every decorative item photographed for this book, nor could all of the designers be identified. Many of these items are available by contacting:

Ruby & Begonia, 204 25th Street, Ogden, UT 84401

(801) 334-7829 • (888) 888-7829 Toll-free

e-mail: ruby@rubyandbegonia.com

Web site: www.rubyandbegonia.com

Every effort has been made to ensure that all information in this book is accurate. However, due to differing conditions, tools, and individual skills, the publisher cannot be responsible for any injuries, losses, and/or other damages, which may result from the use of the information in this book.

This volume is meant to stimulate decorating ideas. If readers are unfamiliar or not proficient in a skill necessary to attempt a project, we urge that they refer to an instructional book specifically addressing the required technique.

For information about custom editions, special sales, premium and corporate purchases, please contact Sterling Special Sales Department at 800-805-5489 or specialsales@sterlingpub.

Library of Congress Cataloging-in-Publication Data

Designer scrapbooks-- the Red Hat Society way / Ruby RedHat ; foreword by Sue Ellen Cooper.
    p. cm.

 Includes index.

 ISBN 1-4027-2000-9

1. Photographs--Conservation and restoration. 2. Photograph albums. 3. Scrapbooks. I. Cooper, Sue Ellen. II. Red Hat Society.

TR465.D47 2005

745.593--dc22

                   2004030190

10 9 8 7 6 5 4 3 2 1

Published by Sterling Publishing Co., Inc.

387 Park Avenue South, New York, NY 10016

©2005 by Sue Ellen Cooper

Distributed in Canada by Sterling Publishing

c/o Canadian Manda Group, 165 Dufferin Street

Toronto, Ontario, Canada M6K 3H6

Distributed in Great Britain by Chrysalis Books Group PLC, The Chrysalis Building,

Bramley Road, London W10 6SP, England

Distributed in Australia by Capricorn Link (Australia) Pty. Ltd.

P. O. Box 704, Windsor, NSW 2756, Australia

Printed and Bound in China

All Rights Reserved

Sterling ISBN 1-4027-2000-9

Ode to the Red Hat Society

A poet put it very well. She said when she was older,
She wouldn't be so meek and mild. She threatened to get bolder.
She'd put a red hat on her head and purple on her shoulder.
She'd make her life a warmer place, her golden years much golder.

We read that poem, all of us, and grasp what she is saying.
We do not need to sit and knit, although we all are graying.
We think about what we can do. Our plans we have been laying.
Instead of working all the time, we'll be out somewhere playing.

We take her colors to our hearts, and then we all go shopping,
For purple clothes and hats of red, with giants brims a-flopping.
We're tired of working all the time, and staying home and mopping.
We order pies and chocolate fudge, and rich desserts with topping.

We crown ourselves as duchesses and countesses and queens.
We prove that playing dress up isn't just for Halloween.
We drape ourselves in jewels, feathers, boas, and sateen.
We see ourselves on television and in magazines.

We laugh, we cry, we hug a lot. We keep each other strong.
When one of us goes out for fun, the rest all go along.
We gad about, we lunch and munch, in one big happy throng.
We've found the place where we fit in, the place we all belong.

©2004 Sue Ellen Cooper and The Red Hat Society, Inc.

Table of Contents

Beforeword

It Began with a Hat

"We believe silliness is the comedy relief of life, and since we are all in it together, we might as well join red-gloved hands and go for the gusto—together."

—Sue Ellen Cooper, Founder and Exalted Queen Mother

Red Hat Society

*I*f we weren't all destined to get older, the Red Hat Society would have never come to be. The last thing Sue Ellen Cooper set out to do was change the world's views on aging. But she has done just that, making thousands of friends along the way.

A number of years ago, Sue Ellen impulsively bought a bright red fedora at a thrift shop, for no other reason than it was cheap and, she thought, quite dashing. A year or two later she read the poem "Warning" by Jenny Joseph, which depicts an older woman in purple clothing with a red hat. She decided that her birthday gift to her dear friend, Linda Murphy, on her 55th birthday would be a vintage red hat and a copy of the poem. She has always enjoyed whimsical decorating ideas, and thought the hat would look nice hanging on a hook next to the framed poem.

Linda embraced the gesture and the red hat. When mutual friends heard about the gift, they too wanted to join in the fun. The beloved birthday gift was given to a handful of girlfriends who shared in this delightful approach to aging.

So what's a gal with a great hat to do? Why, go out of course!

It occurred to these friends that they were becoming a sort of "Red Hat Society" and that perhaps they should go out to tea...in full regalia.

They shopped consignment stores for purple dresses that didn't go with their red hats to complete the picture the poem painted.

The tea was a smashing success. Soon, each one thought of another woman or two she wanted to include, and they bought more red hats. Their group swelled to 18, and they began to encourage others to start their own chapters (more than 18 women don't fit well around a tea table). One of their members passed along the idea to a friend in Florida, and their first "sibling" group was born.

A feature in a national magazine was followed by a newspaper article, which was picked up and published in newspapers around the country, igniting what has developed into a woman's movement. Word continues to spread like wildfire as Red Hatters span the globe, celebrating their 50-plus years within a sisterhood that no one could have ever planned.

Many red hats later and a purple wardrobe to match, the gift Sue Ellen Cooper (top) gave her friend, Linda Murphy (bottom), literally ignited a women's movement named the Red Hat Society.

Sue Ellen was declared Exalted Queen Mother, although she insists anyone who wants to be Queen can appoint herself one too. Her first official edict was, "The rules are there are no rules." Actually, there is one rule: One must be over 50 to wear a red hat and purple clothing. Women under the magic age are welcome to join in the fun by wearing a pink hat and lavender attire. Name your chapter whatever you please, appoint yourself to whatever job you like—just don't take yourself too seriously. As a result there are thousands of Duchesses and Ladies, and as many innumerably preposterous names as there are women in the Red Hat Society.

The ranks of the Red Hat Society have swelled to nearly a million and counting every day.

A friendship that has seen many hairstyles and fashions through the years was the foundation of the "disorganization." As Linda moved to different parts of the country, it was not long before Sue Ellen boarded a plane for a visit. In 1985, the two reconnected in Virginia.

Foreword

A Lifetime of Memories
Even if they are still in a box!

"Recall it as often as you wish, a happy memory never wears out."

—Libbie Fudim

Those who have met me in my "golder" years know a much more free-spirited person than when I was younger. I am a recovering perfectionist and, based on my antics of late, I must be far less concerned with what others think of me.

I am trying to revise my outlook in many areas of my life, especially when it comes to packing my bags for guilt trips. One of the nasty guilt hang-ups I have abandoned is whether I will ever be caught up journaling and scrapbooking my family's photos.

Frosty joins me just about wherever I go. When I sit down to work on scrapbook pages he is always right beside me.

In the past, I struggled with infinite shame if my children's school portraits were not in chronological order in coordinating photo albums. Photos in a few albums is about as far as I got in between carpool duty, managing children's schedules, making nightly dinners, and running my own small business. My dirty little secret was that Mrs. Perfect was accumulating piles and piles of snapshots, negatives, children's drawings, and report cards. Someday, I thought, I would get to them.

In the course of working on this book I was reminded how wonderful it is to have visible souvenirs of my past, infallible memory aids of my family's establishment and growth. The time spent browsing through the Cooper family pictures and photos of early Red Hat fun is always an almost sacred experience for me.

No doubt you feel the same way about your family pictures. But the truth is, for many of us, these treasures are still in those boxes.

One of my favorite pastimes as a devotee of antique and "junque" stores is what led me to finally get around to working on my own scrapbooks. I have often felt a twinge of sadness when I see old photos for sale, sometimes in fancy frames, sometimes just heaped in jumbled, dusty shoeboxes. I wonder how they came to be there.

Who was that little girl hugging the annoyed cat wearing the doll dress and bonnet? What happened to that oh-so-young-looking couple sitting straight and solemn for their formal wedding portrait? Did they have a good life together? Did they raise a family?

Even though I will never know who these people were, I instinctively know that someone, somewhere once considered these photos treasures. I found myself determined that my family's photos would not be abandoned years from now because no one had any idea who we were. It took these orphaned photos and a little nudge from Miss Ruby RedHat (more about her in a minute) to get me going.

Being deeply loved by someone gives you strength; loving someone deeply gives you courage.
—Lao Tzu

All Jewels & Gems

I consider all of our family pictures to be precious jewels, and strictly follow that analogy; some are rubies, others are emeralds. Then there are the diamonds, not so much because they were artfully composed or taken on extra-special occasions, but just because looking at them now elicits a host of recollections that I might otherwise have forgotten.

Looking at certain photos of my son, Shane, and daughter, Andrea, as babies brings back vivid memories of their small bodies and the smell of baby soap on their skin.

There are pictures of their first days of kindergarten, taken four years apart, each child standing straight and tall and holding a brown snack bag. These images remind me of shopping for school shoes, squirting glass cleaner on Shane's tiny glasses, and carefully parting Andrea's hair into ponytails and tying strands of colored yarn around each one.

The photo of Allen (in a huge sombrero) and me on a trip to Puerto Vallarta reminds me of the moustache he wore for years and how scratchy his kisses were.

Then, seemingly in the blink of an eye, there are the children's high school and college graduation photos and wedding pictures.

When I look at the photo of Andrea and husband Matt's first dance as man and wife, I can hear the Bee Gees singing "How Deep is Your Love?" When I look at the photo of Shane and wife Nicole, taken the first time he brought her home to introduce her, I hear him saying, "Mom, I think I love her."

I can't help but smile when I see a photo of Andrea and I hugging at the surprise 49th birthday party she threw for me. On my head is a paper and foil crown that went with all of the other "queenly" decorations. You guessed it—the theme of the party was royalty. This was long before the Red Hat Society began, but who knows, maybe that party planted a seed.

In 1996, before the Red Hat Society formed, Linda was behind the wheel of a convertible with Sue Ellen, her sisters, a cousin, and a friend, showing promise of future antics ahead.

Linda models the very first Red Hat T-shirt in 2000.

When I refer to "family" pictures, I am including those special friends whom we have chosen to be "family." That is what Allen and I have done with Esteemed Vice Mother Linda Murphy and her husband, Bob, known affectionately as the Red Baron. Our families have been friends for more than 25 years, and we sure have the photos to prove it. Our special relationship has survived their moves over the years, from California to New Jersey to Virginia, back to California, and now to Florida.

Ready to Scrap the Ruby Way

*H*ow wonderful that we have photos taken here and there, as the Red Hat Society was born and began to grow. There is Linda modeling the first-ever Red Hat Society T-shirt in front of the coffee shop where we always met for breakfast before church on Sundays (we had no idea what was ahead).

There are so many photos of our early chapter gatherings, and it is interesting to see how our regalia became more and more inventive as time passed.

There we are at the first Red Hat Society convention (Chicago), the second (Nashville), and the third (Dallas). Linda and I have kept many behind-the-scenes photos from the conventions and book tours we have been on together. She seems to find particular amusement in photographing the progressively messier state of my suitcase as time goes on.

We all have special friends whom we've come to think of as extended family, and this applies to the women we draw close within our Red Hat Society. The photos we take of each other and our activities—the teas, the parades, the parties—help us remember and relive these best of times we have spent together.

Sometime soon after the Red Hat Society was born, a little gal by the name of Ruby RedHat came to be. Ruby embodies the Red Hat Society spirit. She is a mischief-maker extraordinaire and can be counted on to try just about anything—including scrapbooking. Ruby has appointed herself the Official Hysterian of the Red Hat Society. She has taken it upon herself to document some of the highlights of Red Hatting.

Ruby's way of scrapbooking is as unique as she is. No one bothered to tell her there are guidelines that traditional scrapbookers follow. Even if she knew there were rules, she'd be sure to break them. It is our hope that Ruby's efforts to learn to scrapbook will serve as inspiration and encouragement. Get ready to scrapbook the Ruby RedHat way, and remember, if it isn't fun, why bother?

In friendship,

Sue Ellen Cooper

Sue Ellen

Introduction

The Ruby in Us All

*R*uby RedHat embodies the best parts of all of us. She is high-spirited, curious, fun loving, and caring, exemplifying many of the endearing qualities found among Red Hatters. When it comes to having a good time, she is the first to declare, "Dessert First!" She has kept that part of herself alive as she lives in the moment and enjoys play of all kinds. She is spontaneous and free, and she inspires those same qualities in her friends. Ruby is the official mascot of the Red Hat Society and she often wiggles her way into all sorts of Red Hat happenings.

You will get to know Ruby very well throughout this book, as she offers her observations and Ruby-isms—comical one-liners that only Ruby could proclaim and we all can relate to.

Scrapbooking has become one of Ruby's favorite activities. She has made a few concessions to practicality, though. She saves negatives or makes multiple copies of photographs because, she says, this frees her up to experiment even more. If she really messes up, she can always start over. She says that scrapbooking with her friends has provided her with some of her best playtimes. Even if they wind up producing a less-than-perfect project, Ruby and friends always come away with wonderful memories of playing together, which, after all, is the essence of Red Hatting.

Rules are Meant to be Broken

*W*hen it comes to scrapbooking, messy doesn't matter. As long as you like the results, who cares? This is a time when you can break the rules, and have fun doing so.

The Red Hat Society is proud to have no rules. Chapter events can be anything members can agree on doing. In like manner, the Red Hat Society has no rules about how a chapter scrapbook can be kept or regarding who should keep it. As with everything else we do, we like to keep these things, shall we say, free form.

Eventually at least one chapterette may appoint herself "Official Hysterian" and just start piling up the photos. After all, some of the things we ladies do have to be seen to be believed (and remembered). Our chapterettes have become our second families, and, as such, deserve the special type of documentation that will record their histories.

Our souvenirs of life's travels and experiences document the history of the Red Hat Society "disorganization." Scrapbooks bring special people, animals, and events near to us, reinforce our special connection with them, and infuse our lives anew with meaning. Each photo, ticket stub, or hand written note is a pearl of great price.

As Ruby has learned, scrapbooking gives us one more way to play—while preserving memories at the same time.

Members of The Founding Chapter gather for scrapbooking the very best way—in a group! We share tools, supplies, and, most of all, fun! Ruby cannot be contained to a seat and insists on dancing on the table.

Tools & Techniques

Tools

*I*n addition to photographs, you will need some basic supplies to create your scrapbook pages, including:

Acid-free glue: Liquid glues are great for die-cuts and other small accents. Most are permanent when wet, but when allowed to dry slightly, items can be repositioned. Use glue sparingly.

Chalk pastels: Chalks are used to blend and/or shade around journaling, torn paper, photos, and other accents. They are generally available in pallet form in a variety of colors.

Decorative edge scissors: Scissors come in a variety of styles and give a nice finishing touch to otherwise straight-edge papers.

Decorative papers: Available in wide range of patterns, textures, and hues. Choose papers within the same color family for each scrapbook page.

Die-cuts and stickers: Available in wide range of fun themes, colors, and patterns.

Embellishments: Tags, beads, ribbon, and any other decorative element, especially if it holds sentimental value, can be incorporated into scrapbooking pages.

Eyelet tools: To save wear on your work surfaces, use a self-healing mat. You'll also need a punch, hammer, and eyelet setter. If you plan to use eyelets of varying sizes, be sure to purchase a punch and setter with interchangeable heads to fit the eyelet of your choice.

Foam tape, dots, or squares: A great way to make elements stand out on your pages, foam tape, dots, and squares are available in different thicknesses.

Adhesives include liquid acid-free glue applied with a pen or stick, foam squares or tape, photo tabs, and sticky dots.

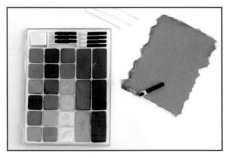

Chalk pastels are easily applied with a small foam brush similar to those used to apply eye makeup.

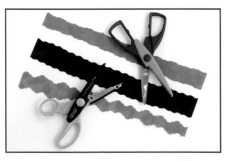

Decorative edge scissors are available in many different patterns.

Glue dots: Small adhesive dots are ideal for attaching metal elements, buttons, and other items that liquid glues won't hold.

Pencil, ruler, scissors

Photo tabs: Can be used to hold photos in place rather than permanently gluing them onto scrapbooking pages.

Tape: To adhere photos, roll tape dispensers are both quick and easy to use. They come in different styles, some with photo tabs, others with double-sided tape. These adhesives are also either permanent or repositionable.

Templates

Scrapbook papers come in a wide variety of colors and textures and are acid free.

Eyelet tools include a self-healing mat, a hole punch with several size heads, an eyelet setter, and a hammer.

Templates make it easy to trace and crop photos or create shapes for mats.

A selection of pencils and markers are scrapbooking staples. Red Hatters may want to include crayons for fun!

Embellishments can include stickers, jewelry, rhinestones, and glitter.

Techniques

When it comes to scrapbooking, Red Hatters believe gaudy is good. We color outside the lines, and freely mix stripes and florals. We tear our papers and leave the perfection to the perfectionists. After all, if you can't have fun doing it, why do it?

There are some basic techniques, however, that will help you get started:

 Adhering ribbon: Tape ribbon ends to back of scrapbook page using acid-free tape (do not use cellophane tape as it's not acid free). You can also use glue or sew ribbon on.

 Chalk pastels: To apply chalk, use small sponge-tip applicator, cotton swab, or your finger. Rub gently; soften effect by brushing with cotton ball.

 Eyelets: To set eyelets, mark your placement with pencil and place self-healing mat under spot. Next, place punch over pencil spot, and lightly tap with hammer. Place eyelet in hole, turn paper over, place eyelet setter in back of eyelet and lightly tap with hammer.

 Photographs: Always use copies in scrapbooks and keep originals separate in acid-free photo boxes or albums. This way, you can experiment with cropping the photo to your heart's content without damaging the original print!

 Tearing paper: There's no need to cut right on lines when it comes to scrapbooking—we'd rather tear! To tear paper, use fingers as guide. Tear in waves, or straight lines. Chalk torn edges if you prefer.

Coloring Outside the Lines

*R*uby set aside an afternoon and assembled enough materials to get started. She gathered a whole bunch of fun stuff—scissors, paint, crayons, glue, stickers, markers, dried flower petals—and piled it on her kitchen table. She planned to compensate for her lack of experience with enthusiasm, which is how she deals with most things she hasn't tried. All those colorful materials—photos, colored papers, sequins, feathers, fabric swatches, stickers—were hers to play with! She experimented with color combinations, mixing and matching patterns that seemingly didn't go with each other.

As she trimmed and glued, she became completely absorbed in what she was doing. Since no one told her that one must be a gifted artist to be a successful scrapbooker, she didn't worry too much about her lack of qualifications. She allowed herself to be transported back to her school days, before she found that she had little artistic talent. By the time most of us have us reached Ruby's age, we have acquired an inner voice of discouragement, a voice that reminds us of all the things we can't do. Ruby doesn't seem to have one of those nagging inner detractors. Or, if she does, she apparently pays little attention to it.

Inspired by the outings of Red Hatters, we came up with scrapbook pages and projects that reflect the colorful antics and zestful spirit of our chapterettes.

Anyone Can Do It

*S*illiness is serious business to Red Hatters. But nothing else needs to be—not if we can help it. Although Ruby became highly intrigued with scrapbooking and expressed sincere appreciation for the talent and creativity of the Official Hysterians of other chapters, she never wasted a moment worrying about whether she could produce something as wonderful on her own. That's just not in her nature.

Ruby knows that while the end result may be important, the journey getting there can be just as extraordinary.

So gather some of your chapterettes, haul out the crayons, colored papers, and glue, and have a scrapbooking party. Just remember: Celebrating life is not about perfection; it's about perception. Losing yourself in the joy of the moment will be good for your soul and help you remember the little girl who used to be you!

Chapter One

The Red Hat Society…We're All in it Together

*"We've found the place where we fit in,
the place we all belong."*

*B*eing height challenged, I have found I can sneak in and out of just about anywhere I like. Believe me, I get around. If I told you everywhere I've been I'd have to poke you with my hatpin, so better to let the life-size Red Hatters indict themselves with the facts of their fun. I *will* tell you that Red Hatters are everywhere. Notice how you never see just one? We travel in packs; it's part of the fun.

Speaking of fun, I'm leading this Red Hat scrapbooking adventure just for fun. (Who do you think taught Sue Ellen that if it isn't fun, why bother?) If you are game to join in, here are a few things to keep in mind:

 Work with a friend or a crew: It's a lot more fun to cheer each other on. Just be sure to smile and tell her how great her page is even if you'd never in a million years put it in your scrapbook.

You're always right: Express yourself! There is no right or wrong way to create a scrapbook page—there is only your way.

 Play nice: You may have an embarrassing photo of a Red Hat sister—get her permission before you share it with the masses, or at least be long gone before she finds out you already did.

Keep it fun: The minute anyone in your midst begins to take things too seriously, tell her to put down her scissors and go for a walk while she comes to her senses.

Sunday Hat Sisterhood

Red Hatters Matter

Spare the Words

One photo can say it all! Because red and purple is such a vibrant combination, a single photo has enough color to carry an entire page. Attach bits of ribbon, rick-rack, and other trims with a hot glue gun or sticky dots.

princess baby

play

Cheat When You Can

Take the easy way out. Rickrack trim in two sizes makes a great border without having to cut out all those wavy edges. Use sticky dots to adhere the wider piece and fabric glue for the narrower strand. Pre-cut paper frames are another great shortcut.

SS ACT

BABY
MONDAY FEB. 23

Pink bonnet baby, Joy invited the Class Act Red Hatters to an afternoon ice cream social. She Arrived with her piggy bank, and paid for the group. She fit right in with her crown and beautiful attire. A future Red Hatter for sure!

-February 2004

We're just getting started!

Order of the Drama Queens
Fullerton, California

Be Square

An easy way to create a colorful page (what's not colorful about red and purple?) is to cut squares and rectangles of coordinating papers, piece them together like a puzzle, and glue them onto a 12" x 12" piece of card stock for the background page.

The Wally Stitch
movie premiere
San Pedro, California
August 18, 2004

Queen

23

Calling All Inviteas

*D*on't be put off by how great it looks. Making your own invitation to a Red Hat tea is easy. First, decide what size envelope you would like to use. You are welcome to make your own, but I promised you shortcuts and one is to buy pre-made envelopes. Use the invitation and envelope pictured as an example.

Materials:

Card stock or paper, red and purple striped

Craft glue

Decorative-edged scissors

Die-cut of teapot and teacups

Glitter pen

Polka dot paper, red

Seed beads, red and clear

Small feather, red

Envelope shown is A2 specialty envelope 4⅜" x 5¾". Measure width of envelope, in this case, 5 ¾". Subtract ⅛". Use equation for height of invitation. 5¾" − ½" = 5¼".

Measure height of envelope, in this case, 4⅜". Subtract ½". Use equation for width of invitation. 4⅜" − ½" = 4¼". Multiply measurement by 3. 4¼" x 3" = 12¾".

Cut piece of polka dot paper 12¾" wide by 5¼" tall. Fold and score width of paper in thirds. Take right-hand third and fold in half and score. Repeat with left-hand side. Open paper and measure 1¾" from bottom right edge of paper. Make a small pencil mark at spot.

Using decorative edge scissors, cut from first right-hand fold to pencil mark. Turn scissors and cut from point at top edge of top fold. First fold will resemble half a kite. Repeat process on far left edge, only this time work from top. (First cut is from first left-hand fold to 1½" from top.) Fold far right and far left panels so wrong side of paper faces out.

Cut piece of striped paper 3⅜"x 1¾". Trim top and bottom edges at angle. Embellish edges with glitter pen. Glue this piece to outside of left-hand flap. Glue feather to flap and add die-cut embellishments. Add seed beads to image with craft glue.

Do you suppose leprechauns felt they were getting a run for their money when they spotted this gang? Thin ribbons can be tied in different configurations and held in place by gluing ends to the back-side of the page. For smaller ribbon designs, tuck ends behind an embellishment on the page.

friends

Friends are the best collectibles.

Red Spread Sandstoners

Vacationing in Ireland-making memories, laughing lots, and having fun, fun, fun.
May 2004

26

Project

Place Card Panache

*O*nce you gather the gals, have some fun decorating place settings with name cards. Cut red cardstock and fold it over to create a tent, and then embellish it to suit your fancy.

Rubber stamps are a fun way to do lettering. Decorate edges by threading thin craft wire through holes made with a sharp knife or scissors.

Add a bead each time you make a loop. Glue a button or use sealing wax to hold a feather in place.

Adding a decorative red hat pin makes a great take-home gift that can be worn long after the party is over.

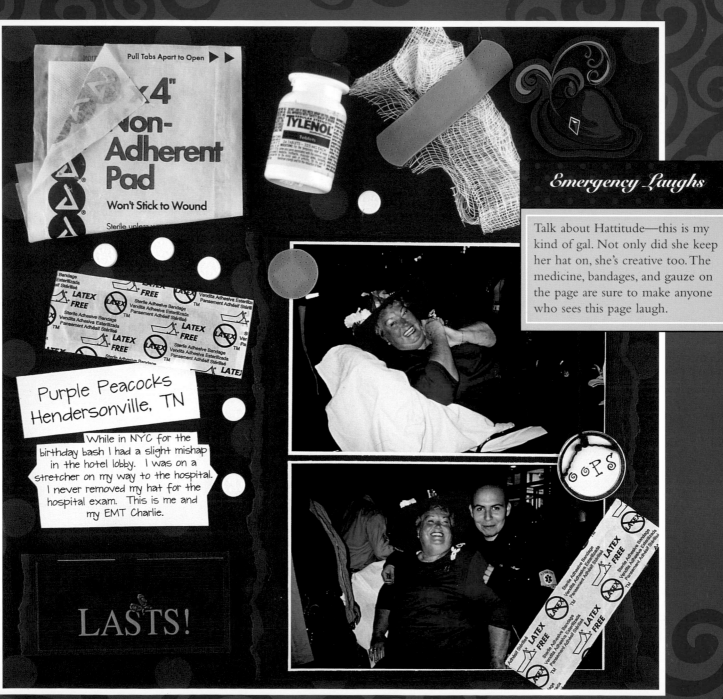

Pull Tabs Apart to Open ▶▶

4"
Non-
Adherent
Pad

Won't Stick to Wound

Sterile unless...

TYLENOL

Emergency Laughs

Talk about Hattitude—this is my kind of gal. Not only did she keep her hat on, she's creative too. The medicine, bandages, and gauze on the page are sure to make anyone who sees this page laugh.

Purple Peacocks
Hendersonville, TN

While in NYC for the birthday bash I had a slight mishap in the hotel lobby. I was on a stretcher on my way to the hospital. I never removed my hat for the hospital exam. This is me and my EMT Charlie.

LASTS!

OOPS

An easy way to make a decorative border is to tear a 12" piece of paper into a 2" or 3" strip. Use a hole punch and make holes about 1" apart. Tie small pieces of ribbon and trim through holes before gluing the strip to the page.

NOT TOO SHABBY

Chapter Two

If the Shoe Fits, Buy It!

"We take her colors to our hearts, and then we all go shopping."

A girl can never have too many pairs of shoes, and in the case of Red Hatters, the more colorful the better. No Red Hat Society regalia is complete without the right footwear.

I was recently lounging under a table at a luncheon where "That Girl" Marlo Thomas was a speaker. She said that a gal can never have enough pairs of black shoes. I knew right then she just didn't get it. Why bother with black? It's just plain boring and no fun at all!

The same is true for your scrapbook pages. Banish boring and go for pizzazz. Here are a few ways to add instant glitz to a page:

 A girl's best friend: Glue a few faux diamonds in various spots. Rhinestones work great.

Fluff it up: Add furs and feathers. Why not?

Go for glitz: Costume jewelry adds instant glitz. Never toss out an orphaned earring or a broken pin. It can be just the thing to make a page sparkle.

Use cutout shapes: Coloring books are a great place to find easy-to-trace shapes such as shoes.

Speaking of fur, you'll notice if you take a close look at me in my everyday attire that I've given up high heels and strappy shoes. What's the point of pinching when I can be in pink scuffie heaven? The trouble is I move so fast sometimes that I walk right out of them and lose them left and right…

Sole Sisters

Fanciful trims can make a page outrageous. Here a wispy trim with beads matches the spirit of the embellished sneakers. Just like the shoes, this page is all about fun! Check the craft section of large discount retailers for 3-yard packages of inexpensive trims.

Cutting out shapes to adorn a page can be easy if you keep the design simple. The cutout of the button shoes on this page are fairly basic. Dress the shoes up with feather tops and flashy buttons.

Hey! Sue Ellen's wearing my shoes!

friends

accessorize, accessorize, accessorize!

I can't believe it! My favorite pair!

Carrying On

In its first life this was a simple red mesh shopping bag. After a Red Hatcarnation, it's now a shopping satchel. To make your own, remove the standard drawstring and pull a purple ribbon through the pocket at the top of the bag. Tie a knot at each end of the ribbon and add a small pin over each knot. Next, trim the top of the bag and the side seams with sequin trim applied with a hot glue gun. Finally, trim the bottom of the bag with a feather boa.

Floppy Fun

I choose to think of these sandals as spa slippers. Strips of fabric were tied around the plastic thongs and topped off with feathers and a ribbon flower crowned with a sparkly red hat earring. The sides of the slippers are finished with metallic trim attached with a hot glue gun.

Wisecracks

Don't be afraid to put words in a friend's mouth, just be sure she laughs! Conversation bubbles make amusing captions. Rather than using photos from just one event, it can be more fun to group photos by theme.

GAD
ABOUT
When in doubt
ABOUT
GAD

Don't worry, I took them back while she was dancing!

It was worth it just to wear those fabulous purple pumps!

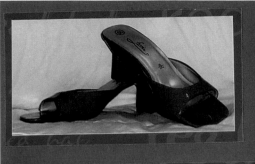

stepping out with

Marti Gilbert, Queen Mother, of the Baxter Babes of Mountain Home, Arkansas, a chapter of the Red Hat Society, is stepping out with Hattitude for their group's first outing.

Heels Up!

Hattitude is much more than a hat—it's coordinating the look from head to toe, and this Red Hatter gets the picture with the perfect shoe page. A simple cutout of a shoe tells the story and a feather dresses it up. The fiber mesh along the bottom of the page is available in small rolls at scrapbook supply stores.

accessorize, accessorize, accessorize!

HATTITUDE

Nutty Napkin Ring

Napkins with handmade napkin rings are sure to bring smiles. This napkin ring is a cinch to make. Cut two strips of paper, one slightly smaller than the other. Glue one strip to the other, and embellish with a lapel pin. Use a sharp object to pierce holes along bottom of papers and thread purple craft wire through holes, bending it into a circle as you go. Add a few beads. Fold the strips back, end to end, punch a hole, and tie with ribbon.

Fancy Footwork Centerpiece

When I first saw this shoe, I thought I was going to be old Ruby RedHat who-lived-in-a-shoe until my guardian, Esteemed Vice Mother Linda Murphy, whispered in my ear that it is actually a centerpiece. Phew! A brown kraft paper shoe available at craft stores was painted red, stamped with some curlicues, and adorned with buttons, sequin trim, feathers, and a ribbon rose.

It's All About ME!

Pebbles in the Sand

If the shoe fits, wear it—or not. After a fairly proper lunch, these gals kicked their shoes off and hit the beach. The pebbles along the bottom of the page bring a day at the shore to life. Small drops of fast-drying glue, like the kind used to mend a broken fingernail, works best with objects like these.

Chapter Three

Red Hatters Exercise Our Funny Bones

"We do not need to sit and knit, although we all are graying."

I gave up worrying about being thin ages ago when I declared, "Round is too a shape!" However, that does not mean Red Hatters have given up exercise. We flex our funny bones often in order to avoid attacks of life-threatening seriousness. Between fits of laughter and regular workouts from trying to pick up where we left off—a common dilemma among women over 50 whether in a red hat or not—I'm working off more than enough calories to justify dessert. It all works out well because I'm the original Eat Dessert First gal.

Here's how keeping those funny bones toned relates to scrapbooking:

 Anything goes: Feathers, tulle, appliqués, jewels, pom-pom fringe, small toys, and even a tiara add fun to a page. If the page gets so filled with fun that it won't fit in a book, display it in a frame or on a small easel.

 Go for glamour: Use glitter and gems—as much as you want.

 Make them laugh: Pull out all the stops. Choose the funniest photos you can find.

 More is more: When it comes to Red Hat Society pages, busy is better so keep adding color and embellishments.

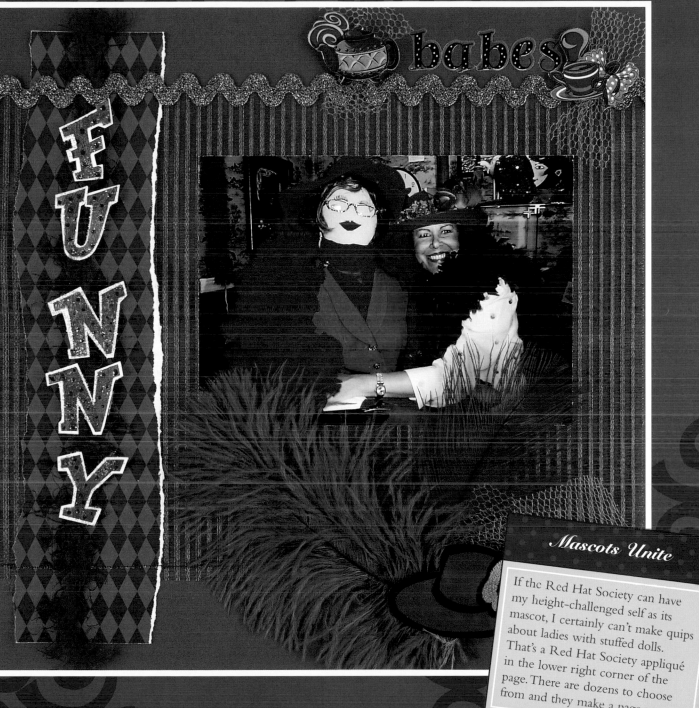

babes

FUNNY

Mascots Unite

If the Red Hat Society can have my height-challenged self as its mascot, I certainly can't make quips about ladies with stuffed dolls. That's a Red Hat Society appliqué in the lower right corner of the page. There are dozens to choose from and they make a page pop.

Foto Frivolity

If you have the right photos—yes, that's Sue Ellen doing the chicken dance in the top left corner—the page is instantly fun and the images tell the story. This page looks great because the background is sedate by Red Hat Society standards, allowing photos to be the focal point.

Speaker Nancy Coey urges fellow
Red Hatters to just "Let it Go!"
Nancy insists that Hatters rise from
their chairs and swing napkins while
repeating the mantra. Here, a ball-
room full of Red Hatters at the
Dallas convention is in full surrender.
The same holds true in your scrap-
booking—let it go and have fun!

THE

red hat Rodeo

Dallas
2004

Project

Show and Tell All

*B*eing a bit of a show off, I carry photos of my Red Hat Society outings so I can brag. Because everyone is so eager to see what my chapterettes and I are up to, I decided to create a small portfolio to preserve my photos.

Materials:

1 lavender brad

2 lavender rivets

6" straw mesh, red

8" decorative string or ribbon

28" pom-pom fringe, red

Craft wire pliers

Flat beads with alphabet letters

Heavy cardstock, 13" x 5"

Illustration such as moi, Ruby

Metal-rimmed shipping tag

Eyelet setting kit

Rubber stamp set and ink pad

Silk flower petals

Fold cardstock in half width wise and score it. Go to town decorating front and back any way you like. Here red ball fringe is used for top and bottom border. Add straw mesh. Stamp tag and tie it to the mesh. Add beads strung on craft wire. Push brads through small slit in paper to hold flower petals in place. Tie decorative string or ribbon through eyelet on front and back edge of card to hold it shut. Violá! You're ready to brag away.

Technique

Setting an Eyelet

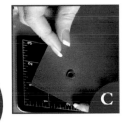

Begin with an eyelet setting kit available at scrapbook supply and craft stores (A). It should include a protective mat, hole punch with various size heads, eyelet setter, and a hammer. Use the hole punch and hammer to make a hole the correct size of the opening needed for the eyelet you are working with (B). Insert eyelet through hole (C). Turn paper over and use eyelet setter and hammer to set eyelet (D). When eyelet is set, insert decorative ribbon or ties as suits your project (E).

Liz Crowborne

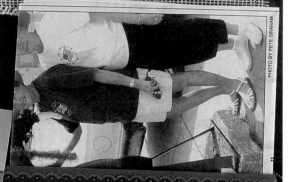

PHOTO BY PETE GRAHAM

Loess Hills
Red Hats

Word Play

Red Hatters love to play with any-thing—including words. Here the name of a women's clothing line is given a little twist and becomes Liz Crowhorne. If you are having trouble being witty, brainstorm with Red Hat Society friends. When you put your hats together you are sure to come up with captions that will bring a smile.

Jokebook

*H*ave you heard the one about…uh-oh, forgot the punch line. Sound familiar? I can never remember the best part of all the good jokes I've heard. After making notes of practical things my whole pre-Red Hat Society life, I realized it was time to start jotting down my favorite belly laughs.

This little joke book is a snap to make. A trip to what used to be called the five-and-dime will get you started. Pick up a small paper pad in the stationery section and decorate the front just as you would a scrapbook page. It's the perfect size to drop into your pocketbook, and the next time you hear a good joke you can write it down.

After a few note-taking sessions, you'll be leading the funny-bone exercises yourself!

The Red Hat Society

The convention was a huge success. We really enjoyed Pasadena. Mary Voight, Kathy Sullivan, Susanne Phillips and I posed for this picture just before the parade. What fun it was to march in the parade. We were all really tired afterwards and meet in the hotel commons area for wine and cheese.

Stick 'em Up!

Use pre-made scrapbook elements such as small tags or make your own easily with a small paper cutter. Whichever you choose, add stick-on lettering, feathers, rhinestones, and trims to personalize the page. Tags can be attached with metallic thread tied through small eyelets.

special

adventure

play

Coronets for Cronies

We crown ourselves as duchesses and queens, we even crown a page. Yep, that's a tiara up there in the corner. Use sticky strips of adhesive to adhere it to the page. The tiara can easily be removed if it needs to be called into action for a royal good time.

MY SISTER

Red Hatters Matter

party

49

Chapter Four

Red Hatters are Damsels in De-Stress!

*"We laugh, we cry, we hug a lot.
We keep each other strong."*

Ladies, ladies, ladies, we must show the world that it's not a competition to see who's the most uptight. It won't be easy, but we can witness to one stressed-out woman at a time. As with most reformation movements, it's best to lead by example and I'm happy to lead the charge.

Let them see us showing our colors in restaurants, theaters, and parades across the land. When they see our red hats bobbing along, they'll know we are serious about de-stressing and they may be inclined to join in. A smile is contagious, and I have yet to meet anyone who doesn't look better with a grin on her face.

Carry the fun forward with scrapbook pages that speak of frivolity and fun. There are dozens of ways to do this, here are just a few:

All the trimmings: Use trims with lots of fringe and texture.

Drop the scissors: Sometimes it's just too much work to cut. Tear papers instead.

Mish-mash match: Mix and match papers for colorful backgrounds.

Shape up: Use fun shapes. Photos can be cut to resemble flowers, or simply cut out the subject and place her picture on the page.

Lovely Lei-dies

A luau party blossomed into a wonderful day, and is fittingly recorded by planting photos of the fun in a paper flowerpot. Photos were cut into the shape of tulips and mounted on bamboo sticks with crochet hearts to resemble the flower's sepal.

memories

Quiet Memories

Sometimes Red Hat fun is a quiet stroll with friends. Double photo mats are easy to make with a small paper cutter and they bring simple photos to life. For a fancy type font on your page, use rub-on words available at a craft store or scrapbook supply retailer.

We have had a Red Hat group in Augusta, KY since May 2004. Augusta is a small town on the Ohio River in Northern Kentucky. Every year on Labor Day weekend we have a festival call Heritage Days. This year our Red Hatters participated in the parade on Saturday.

All Torn Up

Girls on the go don't have hours to spend on one scrapbook page, which is the best part of a design like this. The only cutting is the caption box and the vellum overlay. The rest is done by tearing and gluing a narrow ribbon trim and buttons to the page.

Ruby Reds
of
Arlington
Texas

party

Getting Tipsy

Banish boring! Tipping a photo just a bit, like the one at the lower left, keeps the page from becoming dull blocks of pictures. Tie snippets of ribbon and trim to a piece of paper before mounting it to the page for a quick accent.

Just flitting about

Friends are the best collectibles.

Parasol Party

These Red Hatters are basking in the funshine on a happy day at the beach. A single photo tells the story. The well-composed shot is joined by a purple paper umbrella. Button and bead accents are simple to add and make you want to pick up the parasol and twirl.

Superstar

Reserved Ladies
Red Hat Society
Pawleys Island, South Carolina

Legends
IN CONCERT

Starry Night

These gals don't fool me. They think that just because they named themselves Reserved Ladies, I'm going to believe they behave. Posing with Rod Stewart is not quite up there with sitting home crocheting. Check your gift wrapping supplies for fun page embellishments.

Project

Glass Charms

I don't know about you, but I have a tendency to put a glass down at a party to dance on a table or two and completely forget where I left my drink. Whether your choice of cheer is wine or sparkling water, a glass charm adds to the festivities and keeps everyone drinking out of her own glass rather than mine!

An easy way to make glass charms is to start with a tag key ring available at most stationers. Decorate them with rhinestones, rubber stamps, or bits of paper. It's fun to cut photos in round circles and glue them onto the tags too. Instead of tying the tags to the glass, use colored craft wire and wrap it in fun configurations.

Pink Princesses

Part of evangelizing the world into de-stress mode is teaching our younger Pink Hat sisters the importance of having fun. This group seems to be learning well! The border on the left side of the page is made with decorative scissors and embellished with pink rickrack, and a piece of feather boa. Sprinkle bits of glitter to add sparkle.

Think Pink

I love embossing because it's so simple. All you need is an embossing pen or an embossing ink stamp pad and a heat embossing tool. Write words with the pen or stamp them on the page with the special ink, then shake embossing powder over the lettering. Hold a heat embossing tool a few inches from the page and let it heat the powder until it becomes shiny and raised.

Pink

bonnet

Babes

dEar heArt

Chapter Five

Hats On to Red Hatting!

*"She'd put a red hat on her head and purple on her shoulder.
She'd make her life a warmer place, her golden years much golder."*

With hats firmly planted on our heads, we wear our Red Hat spirit with pride—and I've got pictures to prove it! But I've got news for you gals: None of us are Annie Leibowitz behind the camera. I've got pictures to prove that too. You can only look at so many point-and-shoot photos of a group of Red Hatters at lunch before falling asleep.

Even with a whole lot of effort we may not improve our collective photography skills, but we can sure jazz things up with how we display the photos on a page. Done right, we may be able to look beyond the flaws in the photos and see only the fun and games.

Try some of these tricks to make your scrapbook pages a tribute to Red Hatting:

 Add the unexpected: A curled red pipe cleaner, a piece of tulle, a jewelry pin, an embroidered appliqué, feathers, and other embellishments kick things up a notch.

Be old-fashioned: But just with color. Somehow certain photos look better in black and white. Try printing one or more of your photos in black and white and hand coloring parts of it. I love any excuse to color, don't you?

 Delete dreary details: Cut out distracting backgrounds and boring details. Get your scissors out and trim flawed photos. You'll be amazed how strong you can make a shot when you cut out the distracting stuff.

Make a point: Use fun shapes as a focal point on a page. A bright red hat atop a group photo is sure to offset the chapter lineup.

Cutout for Close-ups

Closely cropping photos ensures that your subjects take center stage, especially when they are cut out.

Hat Stortage

A girl's got to have a hatbox if a girl is going to have hats! Why not make it as personal as you are? The same techniques used in scrapbooking can be used to make a fabulous hatbox.

Materials:

1 yard decorative cord for handle

5" x 7" photograph

Assortment of 12" x 12" scrapbook papers

Beaded fringe

Cording or ribbon, red or purple

Craft glue

Cropping template

Decoupage medium

Embossing heat tool and pen

Embossing powder, purple

Foam paint brush

Glitter and small tip applicator

Hot glue gun

Round hatbox 12" in diameter

Scissors

Small paper roses, several dozen

*P*urchase your hatbox; I found mine at a discount store. Red Hatters love bargains! Remove cord handle threaded through the rivets in box. Pay close attention to how it was put together; you'll have to remember later. A little memory exercise is a good thing!

You can use just about any paper to cover box. Scrap booking paper and wrapping paper work well. Place lid on paper you have chosen for top of box and trace circumference; cut out circle. Choose favorite photo and, using cropping template, cut opening large enough for image to show through. You may want to embellish edges of opening with glitter. You can also add lettering with marking pen or embossing system.

Using craft glue, affix photo to top of box and glue round paper over it. Carefully smooth out air bubbles and wrinkles in paper. Write a caption or sentiment. Using foam brush, apply several coats of decoupage medium to top of box. Continue to smooth any wrinkles. Set lid aside to dry.

Measure height and circumference of box; cut paper to fit. You may have to use several pieces of paper to make it all the way around. Glue paper to box with craft glue and embillish.

Once lid is dry, add beaded trim and small paper flowers around edge with hot glue gun. Don't forget the handle, because a Red Hatter is a girl on the go and her hat needs to come along too. Thread red or purple cord or ribbon back through holes in box to replace cord you removed.

Lady Nancy

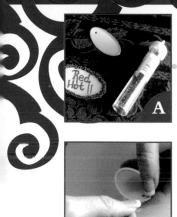

A

F

Project

Beaded and Embossed Tag

Materials:

Double stick tape, thin

Embossing pen, red

Embossing powder, red

Glass seed beads, red

Heat embossing tool

Vellum metal-rimmed tag

Begin with a simple vellum metal-rimmed tag purchased at a scrapbook supply store (A). Apply thin double-stick tape to metal rim (B). Remove backing from tape (C) and apply decorative glass beads (D, E, and F). Use red embossing pen for lettering (G). Sprinkle with red embossing powder (H). Remove excess powder (I) and use heat embossing tool to set design (J).

B

C

D

E

F

G

H

I

J

Project

Stitched Tag

Materials:

Decorative edge scissors

Embossing pen, red

Glue stick

Ink pad, red

Manila shipping tag

Paper, dark red

Pencil

Rhinestone, red

Rubber stamp set

Scissors

Sewing machine or handheld machine for crafting

Small feather, purple

Velour paper, deep red and purple

Wallet-size photo

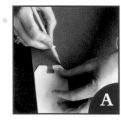

Trace manila shipping tag on red paper (A). Cut paper to size of tag (B) and affix paper to tag with glue stick (C). Trim photo to fit tag (D). Use a dab of glue to affix photo to tag. Even though you'll be sewing all three together, this prevents paper and photo from slipping while you are working.

Use a sewing machine straight stitch to sew the paper and photo to tag (E and F).

Print royal moniker of the Red Hatter on a smaller rectangle of contrasting paper with rubber stamp (G). Position rectangle where you prefer on tag, tuck a feather behind it, and sew to tag (H). Add rhinestone as finishing touch.

Project

Trading Cards

*S*ome of the Red Hat Society elite (that would be everyone) have taken to swapping trading cards with their Red Hat names, photos, and a few essential tidbits about themselves. The guys can keep their baseball cards; these are much more attractive. Trading cards can be a hoot to haggle over, but once you get your collection complete, consider carrying them in a brag book.

Materials:

¼" hole punch

Narrow ribbon in several colors

Small jump rings

Trading cards

Punch holes in tops and bottoms of cards and add eyelets. Attach to each other with small jump rings. Tie bits of ribbon and trim to rings to add some whimsy.

Carry trading cards tied with pretty ribbon, and the minute one of the sisters tries to one-up you with who she's met, untie the ribbon and let your collection drop open. Say no more—you're a well-traveled Red Hatter.

The Red Hat Society of New Canton (Red Hat Pins) walked in the parade on Saturday, along with the Red Hat Society from Barry, and the Red Hat Pins (pictured on the left) from New Canton kept the crowd well entertained after the parade . . . complete with a fashion style show and kazoo concert. What a blast! These ladies know how to have a good time!

"Dapper Dan Little and Regal Ralph Garner were our escorts, decked out in fine tuxes from Shirl's Sew Shop in New Canton," said Pauline Little.

oh   when   the

Anyone Can Kazoo!

When it comes to a musical instrument, the obvious choice is a kazoo. This two-page spread shows our popularity at parades and important community events. Have fun cutting out different Red Hatters in action and be sure to include local newspaper coverage.

Parade Winners

Antiques - 1st, Kinderhook State Bank; 2nd, Kevin Wok. Clowns - 1st, Chris Sutton as Sparkles (his 11th yr. in this parade); 2nd, Well's clowns. Participation Awards - Karmon's Dance Academy. Organization or Group - 1st, Over 80 Red Hats; 2nd, New Canton Red Hat Pins 3rd, Barry Red Hats; and 4th, Methodist Church. Novelty - 1st, Dean Coleman; 2nd, Lonnie Wells. Families or Individuals - 1st, Cincinatti Landing Pirates; 2nd, Shirl's Sew Shop. Tractors - 1st, Richard Patton; 2nd, Bill Bigsby; 3rd, Tiger Wells. Horses - 1st, Longhorn rider. Drawn Rigs - 1st, Karen Harper; 2nd, Wendell Garner.

Hats go Marching in

Ring in the Joy

Each theme phrase is held to shaggy yarn with small jump rings threaded through rivets. The lettering is done with a computer.

Chapter Six

We're Resting, Not Rusting!

"We're tired of working all the time, and staying home and mopping. We order pies and chocolate fudge, and rich desserts with topping."

*A*fter surviving years of hot flashes, which I choose to call "my own personal summers," I have taken to breaking a sweat only when it's absolutely necessary. I'm doing my best to see how Lady Leisure and her Ladies Who Lunch live. Don't get me wrong; I am having a blast—just on my own terms. I like a little golf, a little bingo, and some bowling once in awhile. (I hide behind the pins and dodge the ball, it's so fun!) Occasionally I parachute from an airplane or enter a beauty contest, but there are days that rest is best.

On a rare down day, I like to relive a particularly fun day and scrapbooking is a great way to laugh all over again. I've become pretty good at it, at least by my short standards. I am only too happy to be the first to speak up and share more ideas for scrapbooking fun:

 Bring photos to life: If there is something in the photo that you can recreate on the page, do it! A miniature evergreen tree for the holidays or a pair of champagne glasses with a party scene make a page scream Red Hat style.

 Make me a star: I love being included in everything, so feel free to incorporate an image of me on the page. I am up for just about anything; just be sure I am having fun!

 Remember, boring is bad: Think before you stick. Arrange photos several different ways before you adhere them to the page. If you are going to use more than three photos on a page, stagger and tilt them so the arrangement is visually interesting.

 Simple surprises: Use unexpected objects on pages. If the subjects are playing a game, for example, use game pieces or other dimensional objects on the page.

Tee Time Fun

Golf has always been a challenge for me. The ball is almost as big as I am. These gals had a ball. In fact, that's them in the ball. The giant club tells a great story of a day of miniature golf.

FUN

play.

Time to play...
The Red Hat way

The Shady Ladies of
Salida California
playing miniature golf.

giggly girls

1. Countess Marie Geers, Lady Nita Arnold, Princess Pat Bengfort, & Contessa Anna Ubaldini.

2. Queen Sue Frankel reads the "vows" as a new member pledges the sisterhood while her sponsor stands with her.

3. Tables for six give enough room to spread out and play Bingo.

4. We used Bingo as the theme for our luncheon. (Note the red hat stickers in the center of the Bingo card).

5. Guest Jane Farrington (Sue Ellens sister), Lady Louise DiMarco, & Lady Lee Collins.

Fun by the Numbers

A bingo party can be remembered fondly when it's kept alive on scrapbook pages. Captions assure we remember who was there. The photos are coded to the captions with clever stickers in an old type-writer font.

RENIOR RED HATS
TUSTIN, CALIFORNIA

BINGO

B	I	N	G	O
7	30	32	50	64
5	21	43	51	65
8	28		48	73
12	29	35	49	75
3	20	41	59	72

I 50 — Bingo!

A vintage bingo card and game pieces bring the game out of the photo and onto the page. I'm an unabashed name dropper, so I'll point out Jane, Sue Ellen's sister, known as Prin-Sis, is above on the left.

December 2003

R

Our decorated Christmas Tree for our city's annual tree contest. We made Red Hat ornaments out of foam, embellished with lace, jewels, buttons and feathers. Our garland was made of dried orange slices, cranberries, and popcorn. We won first place and were awarded a pizza party at a local restaurant. We had such a great time.

December 2003

The Season for Folly

Red Hat Society trees seem to pop up everywhere come November and December. The little tree atop this page is just my size. The red hat ornaments are part of a bracelet and the little balls and mini-tree decorations can be found at craft stores.

Sweater Ornaments

*I*t may look like a tree ornament to you, but I have my eyes on these fabulous sweaters to wear to Red Hat Society holiday parties. I have such a time with clothes, so if I see something in the right size, I have to grab it when I can.

This sweater on the left is the height of fashion with its jeweled RHS charms, ribbon belt, and fabulous doodads. The sweater was purchased in the doll-making section of a craft store. On the right is the very vogue shaggy yarn look. It might be a good style for me because I can hide an extra dessert or two when wearing it.

It's made by cutting out a piece of cardboard in the shape of a sweater and wrapping it with purple furry yarn. A piece of red yarn makes a scarf.

That's it, I'm out of here. I've always known I was a real doll; I just need to shop like one.

Recipe Cards and Box

*S*omeone once said, "It's all about the food." I couldn't agree more. Personally, I have given up cooking for practicality and only get busy in the kitchen if I am whipping up a treat. That's why even my recipe box and the cards I keep in it have to be fun.

I prefer to use 5" x 7" recipe cards these days—the words can be bigger and easier to read. Use paper cutouts and borders just like you would on a scrapbook page. The fun font on your computer makes a nice header for the cards.

Materials:

> 5" x 7" recipe cards
>
> Buttons and trims
>
> Craft paint, red and purple
>
> Embroidered appliqués
>
> Foam paint brush
>
> Foam stamps
>
> Hot glue gun
>
> Stick-on letters
>
> Unfinished wood box with lid, at least 5" x 7"

Paint box with red craft paint and stamp designs with foam stamps and purple paint. Apply buttons, appliqués, and yarn with hot glue gun. Use stick-on letters to label box or to make a whimsical message.

For a fun party, send sister Red Hatters blank cards with instructions to decorate them and to include favorite recipes. Exchange cards at your next meeting. Everyone will leave with a full box of recipies.

*Tacky is okay,
gaudy is positively
good!*

Toast to Fun

Miniature glasses can be found in
the wedding section of a craft store.
A toy store is a good source too,
and what an outing that could be!
Prowling the aisles in search of
scrapbooking ideas, you'll surely
turn some little heads!

Last Spring our group was invited to the University of Virginia to test the "Intelligent Walker". It was fun and a great privilege for our Rockin' Red Hats to be able to help scientific and medical research in this important endeavor.

Think Outside The Hatbox

reducation

Dimensional Doodads

The Rockin' Red Hats were asked to participate in the research and development of a new walker. The small lights on the subject surely had some serious meaning, but I thought I was pretty witty to cover myself with miniature white pom-poms and offer my services.

Chapter Seven

We Take Our Silliness Seriously!

"We think about what we can do. Our plans we have been laying.
Instead of working all the time, we'll be out somewhere playing."

$\mathcal{S}$eriously, let's be silly. It's much more fun. I've spent far too much time being somber about too many things and it's time to put some energy into fun.

I'm going to march in a parade. Get up and dance. Sit on a throne for tea and live out the playtime dreams of my girlhood. Speaking of girlhood, remember art class in grammar school? We used Popsicle sticks to spread paste, played with finger paint, and used crayons with reckless abandon. It was all about fun, and if necessary, making a mess.

I give you permission to go back to your art classes of long ago. As a Red Hat Society scrapbooker, imagine yourself as that little girl who never worried about what someone else thought of her work. The only thing to take seriously is being silly. Here's how to have seriously silly scrapbook fun:

 Focus on fun: Crop boring backgrounds or dead areas of photos and show only good, tight shots of fun and frivolity.

 Play with toys: A small toy can add to the story on your scrapbook page. Use it to embellish whatever you like.

 Raise it up: Use foam squares to lift images and artwork from background page for dimension.

Use word play: Red Hatters love to play with everything, including words. Go for the pun and create alliterations; whatever it takes to make page captions fun.

The throne at a Red Hat Society tea is immortalized with a miniature toy chair all gussied up and glued to the page along with a photo line-up of women in search of a very good time.

Scarlett O'Hatters
Frankfort, KY

It's never too late

Helping Holiday Hatters

82

Frivoli-trees

Take Time for Tease

Whether you gather for tea or for tease, word play in captions is sure to bring a smile. On this page are Red Hat Christmas trees decked with balls of jolly!

The Mint Juleps of Castle Pine
est. March 9, 2004

We celebrated Red Hat Day in style by having the Red Hatters—who all live on Castle Pines Street in Montgomery, Alabama—decorate their doors with Red Hat wreaths. The Mint Juleps of Castle Pines are proud to be members of the Red Hat Society.

Grand Prize Winner
Patsie Demo

1st Place
Betty Messick

2nd Place
Sandra Perrett

3rd Place
Judy Taylor

Healthy Hang-Ups

Door pride! These Red Hatters participated in a door decorating contest and entries ranged from traditional to flamboyant. Each one is different, so photos were pulled together with a cute-as-a-button treatment that attaches captions.

Project

Jewelry Keeper

*E*very royal Red Hatter needs a place to keep her jewels when she's not holding court. A small jewelry box is the perfect gift to bestow on a special friend or to serve as a party favor at the next hattering.

Materials:

> 2 dozen red buttons
>
> 24" red trim
>
> Craft paint, purple
>
> Double-stick craft tape
>
> Foam paint brush
>
> Hot glue gun
>
> Ink stamp pad, black
>
> Miniature glass decorative beads, red
>
> Oval cardboard box with lid
>
> Rubber stamp set
>
> Silk rose, large red

Paint inside and outside of box with purple paint and foam brush. Letter favorite words around rim of box top with rubber stamps and black ink. (You can also use rub-on words and lettering available at scrapbook supply stores.) Apply double-stick tape around lower side of box and cover with miniature red glass beads. Using hot glue gun, apply buttons and trim. Crown box with red silk rose.

Project

Invitation

*A*n invitation to a Red Hat Society gathering is a royal order to gather for fun. Handmade invitations can be a precursor to good times ahead.

The first step is to decide what size envelope you would like to use for the finished invitation. Measure and cut a piece of red card stock or paper to the following dimension: height of envelope x 2 – 1" x width of envelope. As an example, if you are using a No. 10 envelope, your paper will be 9 ½" x 7". Remember to allow about ⅛" allowance so invitation can easily slide into envelope.

Use decorative papers and embellishments to decorate front of card however you choose. Mini glass beads add shimmer and shine and are easy to apply with craft or hot glue. Tie invitation with bow and tag that make it clear this is a command performance.

Technique

Easy Beading

*A*pplying glass beads is fast and easy. First, apply double-stick tape to paper (A). Remove backing from tape (B). Sprinkle small red glass beads over tape (C and D). Use fingers to press beads firmly down. Shake off loose beads and return to bottle for future use (E). You'll have a sparkling accent that is a snazzy addition to any paper project (F).

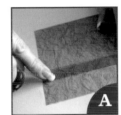

A

D

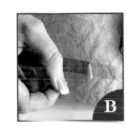

B

E

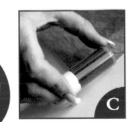

C

F

SHE WHO LAUGHS
LASTS!

Red Pickle Dilly's
Dillsburg, PA

"Cow Parade"
a fiberglass
Red Hat cow

All Buttoned Up

There is no mistaking this bovine beauty for Elsie the Borden Cow—she's a Red Hatter no doubt! Using buttons as a frame for the caption adds a whimsical touch, and matting photos on red paper makes them stand out.

Happy Hulas

The Bloomin' Tea Roses traded red hats for haka leis and took to acting like hulagans. Tipping photos at different angles and using a teacup die-cut for the caption makes the page fun and still lets the superbly silly photos tell a story of Red Hat hula.

Friends are the best collectibles.

Bloomin*
Tea Roses
San Dimas,
California*

We're just getting started!

Chapter Eight

Red Hatters: We're Off Our Rockers!

"When one of us goes out for fun, the rest all go along."

*R*ed Hatters give new meaning to rocking. Banish the thought of creaking back and forth on the porch, watching the world go by. I am nowhere close to the sidelines; I'm ready to rock and roll!

By the looks of what Red Hatters are up to worldwide, I'm in good company. My list of adventures to master is long and I plan to keep checking them off. Whether it's flying a plane, driving a race car, or dancing on the beach, I'm ready to shake and sway.

My scrapbook pages chronicle countless crazy adventures and yours can too. Here's how to make your pages rock right along with you:

 Be fearless: Don't be afraid to cut photos into fun shapes.

 Double the fun: If an event has lots of good photos, work in two-page spreads. Unify the pages with a similar design using die-cuts that mirror each other.

Get tipsy: If you are working with several photos of the same size, tip and tilt them at different angles.

 Make it pop: Use photos with contrasting papers so they jump off the page.

the Classy Lasses of Williamsburg

Babes in Toyland

These gals must have thought they were Red Hatters when rock and roll wannabes paid their table a visit. Small guitars, a radio, and something only a Red Hatter would recognize—LP records—make a page shake, rattle, and roll. Small embellishments can be found in craft stores in the paper section.

Sometimes there is so much mer-riment to record that it can't be contained on one page, so spread out the fun and design facing pages that carry a theme. Wine-glass charms make perfect minia-ture mocktails, and no Red Hatter would hit the beach without her bag and ball!

BUXOM

beach

babes

The Red Hat Tamales

For the title of the page, a rubber stamp was used to apply embossing ink followed by black embossing powder. Once the heat embossing tool created shiny raised letters, the words were trimmed and attached to the page with small brads.

93

A DAY OF

SINGING

&

DANCING

WITH ARTIST & SOLOIST "CHARLES ALEXANDER".

Dancing Queen

Not only is the polka dotted Red Hatter swinging, so is the red paper doll dancer. Dress up a die-cut with a red hat pin, a small bow, and a fancy pipe cleaner skirt. The embellishments at the lower left side of the page are appliqués. The slim white mats help pictures stand out.

Scrapbook Cover

$\mathcal{S}$ue Ellen has a book and so do I—and you can too! Rather than toiling for long literary hours, personalize a scrapbook cover and make it your own.

Start with a good quality album. Chances are good your Red Hat Society friends will be clamoring to flip through the pages, and a poorly made book will not withstand the excitement. Glass beads can be easily applied to frame the photo opening on the cover. Remember, "It's All About Me" (meaning you!), so put your own photo on the cover.

Use craft glue to attach ribbon and trim and foam squares to adhere paper embellishments. Quick-drying craft cement is best for jewelry and small metal decorations.

95

Crazy Hatters bring clean meaning to tying one on. Find tassels like this at a fabric store and add gold metallic thread for pizzazz. Don't be concerned about grouping pictures on a page by outing. If you're off your rockers, that's enough to tie a page together.

PIER ONE THEATRE

KENAI RIVER REDS
(some pinks)...
and we ain't salmon

Decorative Frame

This is a rap you won't want to beat—you'll be happy you were framed. There's no need to defend yourself if someone charges you with having fun.

Get in on the act of breaking the rules. Make your own frame and brag about walking on the risky side of decorum.

Materials:

Assorted strands of ribbon and string

Beads, feathers, and other embellishments

Craft paint, red

Craft wire

Foam paint brush

Hot glue gun

Unfinished wood frame

Paint frame with two coats of red paint; be sure to let dry between applications.

Wrap decorative string with beads around random parts of frame. Add buttons, feathers, and other embellishments with hot glue gun. The Good Old Days plaque is part of a popular line of embellishments. Rather than just gluing plaque to frame, it's more interesting to loop string through holes and glue ends to back of frame.

These are the good old days...I'm going to have to work on getting Carly Simon in a red hat. Let her know I'm looking for her.

Queen Mother Joanne Mitchell and Vice Queen Mother Linda Millinan got together one morning to make a red hat for the Queen Mothers 1950 Chrysler Windsor. The idea came to the queen in the middle of a sleepless night. We spray painted a bushel basket red and then cut a brim from floorcloth canvas also painted red. We decorated the basket with red and pruple silk flowers and attached a large purple organza ribbon. We have driven it many places and plan to drive it everywhere we can go at only 45 miles per hour. That's the top speed that the hat will tolerate!

Joanne's Rouge Chapeau Gang
Ovid, New York

Speed Demons 1

The cops are gonna get her sooner or later 'cuz she can't keep her foot off the accelerator—go granny, go granny, go granny go! (I've been a Jan & Dean fan ever since I can remember.) The cruising purple pleasure car racing along the page had a custom paint job courtesy of some enamel model paint.

Speed Demons 2

The two-lane highway is cut from paper and ties the two pages together. When using repetitive photos, cut some of them out, crop others tightly, and be sure to position them at different angles.

Chapter Nine

Dress for Excess!

"We drape ourselves in jewels, feathers, boas, and sateen. We see ourselves on television and in magazines."

Okay girls, let's go for gaudy. After years of constraining ourselves to matching beige and taupe, let the colors fly bold and bright. Only the brightest reds and brilliant purples will do. Feathers are better and ruffles rule.

Let out the gal you always wanted to be or act the part you never got in the school play. Be the belle of the ball, the bar room babe, hide behind a mask, or don a purple poncho for a Harley ride. Whatever you do, just don't be subtle.

Dress your scrapbook pages with the same enthusiasm as your Red Hat outfits. Here's how:

 Be lavish and layer: Pattern-on-pattern and contrast-upon-contrast is a good design tip when working with papers. Bring on the clash and go for garish.

Bling is best: Use metallic trims and accents for royal shine.

Bright is beautiful: Use vivid, brilliant papers and embellish them with glee.

Fashion a show: Cut out photos of great showmanship and create collages that tell a story.

Just Flitting About

Gaudy Is Good

Fluttering & Flitting

Play up extravagance on the page just like you do with your Red Hat Society wardrobe. Multiple mats under photos add color and patterns, and items such as tulle and shaggy yarns are fanciful.

Outside The Hatbox

Dress for Excess...
We had a great time in Dallas this Spring. The formal Banquet was our Favorite (of course!), We could really Show off our "Hattitude"!

-2003

Layer Upon Layer

Put aside the Easter egg jokes and raise a tray of desserts to this pink princess! She's getting a fine redu-cation. Look closely under the vel-lum message and you'll see a red hat. Layering papers and adding an image under vellum adds the little excess Red Hatters expect.

Dames in Dallas. . . .

There's Fun After Fifty

Red Hat

Dall Hat Society

The Founding Chapter

2004

For Real?!

We all woke up when this pair showed up for breakfast at the Red Hat Society convention in Dallas. Sheer gift bags make great envelopes for holding pictures and keepsakes on a page.

Desert-bound Red Hatters have to be concerned with being red hot lots, so we understand if their gaudiness has to be confined to hats. That doesn't bar plastic beads or rhinestone jewelry. You can place jewelry and other items on a color copier and use copies for embellishments instead of the fabulous fakes.

Just flitting about

1. We had an Easter theme charity lunch. Several members provided the food and we each put in the $15.00 that we usually spend on lunch and gave it to a local charity. 2. This picture is on formal night of our cruise we went on. There were 200 Red Hatters on it. 3. Several members standing in front of a floral arrangement in the lobby of the Mariott Desert Springs Hotel.

Crimson Chicks
La Quinta, California

Journal

So much imagination goes into some of the gaudy Red Hatter get-ups that you may be inspired to take some notes. Journal ideas for dressing up before your next escapade or record your own wardrobe to ensure you don't show up in the same thing twice.

Personalizing a journal is simple. Gather the same supplies you use for scrapbooking and affix your own designs to the cover. A hardcover sketchbook with a spiral binding that's easy to open and flip through can be found at most art supply stores. For an extra accent, tie bits of ribbon and trim to the spirals.

Project

Creating a Bra-Haha

Materials:

1 yard beaded trim, red	Needle and thread, red
1 large bra, red	Purse handle
4" beaded trim, purple	Red Hat charms
6" ribbon, purple	Sewing scissors
Craft glue	Small tassel, red
Hot glue gun	

Start with large red bra; underwire styles work best (A). Cut elastic straps off bra (B). Cut sides of bra (C). Using hot glue gun, turn under raw edges left after removing sides of bra (D).

Hot glue red beaded trim to lower half of bra cup and along underwire (E). Glue two cups together along the bottom edges with the hot glue gun (F). Fold top cup in half, placing flap to inside (G). Tack under with hot glue.

Hot glue red beaded trim to top of back cup (H). Fold over top cup to create purse flap (I). Cut 1½" piece of purple beaded trim. Wrap beaded trim around tassel ¾" from top and glue in place (J and K). Cover edges of beaded trim with narrow purple ribbon and glue in place (L).

Tie tassel through metal strap loop on point of front flap and glue in place (M). Tie several Red Hat charms to purse handle (N). Sew sides of purse to purse handle (O).

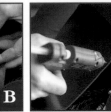

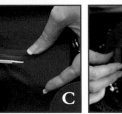

Bra Brag

Yes, it's a lingerie bag of sorts and it's what fashion-conscious Red Hatters are carrying to the season's biggest formal events. There is lots of support for this trend and it won't be long before more women are hooked.

Who's that Model on the Hat Walk?

"Cotton" dress

Beach babe

"Print" dress

The Gambler 97 years old

The Pregnant bride & her Brides-Maid

"40 Carrot" gown

Show-Offs 1

Models on the Paris runways have lots to learn from us. We know how to smile and we have our own style for strutting our stuff. Building a photo collage with cutouts allows for whimsical placement on the page and makes room for many more pictures.

The Red Hat Lakers
Present:
"A Unique Fashion Show"

"Card" party dress

Benefit for L.S.S. Library
Tuesday, July 27
2:00 p.m., Auditorium

"Tea" gown

"Handmade" dress

"Box" suit

"Can-Can" dress

"Drape" dress

"Ho[...] dress

Show-Offs 2

Using an envelope or making a pouch is a great way to keep programs or invitations in place. I only wish an envelope would help me remember other things too. Trimming a photo with metallic thread or trim makes an interesting detail.

Chapter Ten

Red Hatters are Queens for a Day!

"We crown ourselves as duchesses and countesses and queens.
We prove that playing dress up isn't just for Halloween."

There is a bit of a queen in each of us, and now is the time to step up to the throne and court a bit of fun. Pomp and circumstance shall flow from kazoos and a mighty scepter will be bestowed into the royal hand. No House of Lords need be consulted for it is the Ladies of the Society who approve a coronation.

Royal hattenings must be recorded by the Official Hysterian of the chapter or it shall be off with her hat! A certain amount of decorum is called for on the royal pages, for they need to reflect the station of the Queen.

Here are a few redulations for the Queen's pages:

 Crown with glory: Use jewels, rhinestones, and pins to embellish a page. Look for details in photos you can decorate such as the jewel on a crown or the royal ring.

 Gild with gold: Gold and yellow perfectly accent red and purple. Metallic borders add majestic panache too.

 Proclaim your frivolity: If there was an official proclamation or schedule of events, paraphrase it in journal-style captions. Be sure to preserve the details of the festivities.

Spotlight the crown jewels: Find the extraordinary in coronation photos. Was the scepter a toilet plunger? Did the Queen have an imperial robe? Choose photos that record royal ridiculousness.

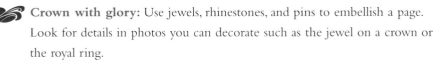

CROWN the Queen

Gaudy Is Good

A Surprise Coronation was held to crown Queen Mum, Rita Drach. Red Foxy Ladies met for a picnic & ended the event by having a full-blow coronation, which included Debbie Blume Crowning our Queen Mum. Her robe was made by Jane Dambauer, crown by Helen Luebbehusen & sash by Barbara Mohr. princesses fanned their Queen with purple plumes as each presented her with special gifts.

—August 2004

Red Foxy Ladies:
Princess sitting; L to R- Joanne Tretter, Jane Dambauer, Queen mum, Mary Nice Jochem, Mary Lou Luebbehusen Standing; L to R- Pearline Wilson, Debbie Blume, Darla Schipp, Helen Luebbehusen & Susie Luebbehusen.

Taken by Surprise

Unlike the coronations of monotonous monarchies, Red Hat coronations are often a surprise. Be sure to get good photos of Her Majesty's delight during a royal ambush. Crop in tight on the Queen, and share the creative details of the day in captions.

The highlight of our June 2004 meeting was the coronation of our new Queen Mum, Janet Curran. She was assisted by her royal ladies in waiting, Sabrina Katzenmeyer, Barbara Reynolds, Helen Champion & Martha Parenica, into a red robe (borrowed from the local high school) and was presented a five strand set of pearls, which must have come from a large oyster, because they hung down to her waist! Swearing on her pearls and red hat, Janet took the oath of office.

Le Fleur _____ is Ohio
_____ Radke, Ladies Waiting: Martha Parenica,
_____ Reynolds, Sabrina Katzenmeyer, Vice Queen
_____ Janet Curran, Founding Queen Mary

Coronation 1

Every Queen deserves her proper place and space, which in the chapter scrapbook may be two pages of the coronation. While a picture is said to be worth a thousand words, the words are important too. Posting the royal oath on the page announces what this chapter expects of Her Majesty.

Do you promise, on your pearls, to give friendship and sisterhood to women who have decided to greet middle age by wearing purple & a red hat?

Do you promise to lead your queen Dom in light-hearted fun and frivolity, encourage them to eat dessert first and occasionally play at the table?

Do you promise to set a good example by always wearing our colors at all official red hat events?

Do you promise to openly frolic with other Red Hatters, to extend a red-gloved hand of sisterly welcome to visiting red hatters?

Do you promise to lead by having no rules as declared by the national headquarters and to give each of your ladies an equal opportunity to plan events and to have a say in how to have fun?

After answering "I Do" to each statement and swearing in, the Royal Ladies in waiting presented Janet with her sparkling tiara, which will fit right on her red hats, and her sash and scepter. Janet then went to each member, calling her by her Red Hat name, anointing her on her shoulder with her scepter and exchanging hugs and words of joy.

our forever young Queen

Next on the agenda, our Vice Queen Marge Prebe agreed to continue as Vice Queen for the next two years. The group helped Marge into her robe then presented her with a vice hat covered with mini playing cards, dice and mini bottles of champagne. Marge then took a vow that she will always keep vice in her life and answered "I Do" to the Vice Queen oath.

Le Fleur Rouge-Macedonia Ohio
L To R-New Queen Janet Curran, founding Queen Mary Buthovic, Vice Queen Marge Prebe

I will greet middle age with verve, humor and enthusiasm.
I will take my silliness seriously, knowing that it is the comedy relief of life.
I agree to join Red-gloved hands with my Red Hatted sisters and go for the gusto together.
I will strive to help create new bonds and strengthen existing bonds among my sisters as we move forward to wherever life takes us next.

Coronation 2

Using a different treatment for each caption keeps the text from being a regal yawner. Captions are set in the same font for continuity, but each one is matted and attached to the page a little differently, which makes the page fun to read.

A royal Coronation

The Bearoness was serenaded with new words to the "Miss America" theme. She was interviewed with a large microphone & was fully dressed as royalty. Proof again that celebrating getting older can be fun!

The Berrestained Bears

forever young

It's never too late to have a happy childhood.

Make Bad Better

Often you may be faced with less-than-fabulous photos from a coronation, so you'll have to resort to graphic elements to give a page zing. Trim photos as tight as possible, and make them different dimensions. Add lots of details such as brads, snaps, trims, and tags.

Royal Scepter

*I*n order to reign, a Queen must have a scepter. The royal treasury need not be raided to provide it. The royal warrant for the scepter is best given to the most creative lady in the queendom for she is sure to come up with an uncommon commission.

Materials:

1 yard thin ribbon, purple	Charms, beads, and trinkets
1 yard thin ribbon, red	Craft paint, purple and red
2 foam paint brushes	Crown pin
3" wood ball	Electric drill
6" metal hook	Feathers, purple
6" sequin trim, red	Hot glue gun
8" wood spindle	Silk rose about 5" in
Appliqués	diameter, red

Paint spindle red and ball purple using foam brushes. Hot glue 6" pieces of red and purple ribbon around top of spindle.

Remove plastic green bottom from red silk rose, flatten, and glue to top of spindle, covering top edges of the ribbons.

Drill small hole in top of wood ball and insert hook. Wrap base of hook with sequin trim and feathers. Thread crown pin through hook.

Hot glue wood ball over silk rose to top of scepter. Tie charms, beads, and pins to ribbons. Decorate scepter with feathers, appliqués, and trinkets using hot glue gun.

Technique

Preparing Pins for Pages

*P*ins make sparkling embellishments and can be easily prepped for use on pages (A). Using small wire cutters (B), remove shank from back of pin. Once shank is removed and back of pin is flat, use a hot glue gun or foam square to affix the pin to the page (C).

Small Photo Album

*W*hen there is an abundance of photos from the royal photographer there needs to be a proper place to keep them. The perfect answer is to customize a photo album for imperial use.

A small photo album is portable and easy for the Queen to take with her on walkabouts. Look for an album with a unique feature such as a brass clasp or lock. Embellish the cover the same way you would a scrapbook page. Stay away from gluing full sheets of paper to a cloth cover; it may wrinkle and crack with wear.

Add ribbons, trims, charms, and beads. A tag inscribed Queen assures that Her Majesty feels she has received her due respect. The book can stay in her possession to be enjoyed for many years.

Waves of Fun

The royal wave would be nothing without a red glove, and during her first book tour, our Exalted Queen Mother perfected the motion. Use an inexpensive glove and create a page that gives the Queen a hand. (Okay, that was even a little too punny for me.)

hattitude   friends

party   sisters

You Bet!

No kingdom is legitimate without its stables and equestrians. These ladies of the court decided to play the horses rather than go for a ride. Use scrapbook paper and decorations to create a pocket for extra photos.

Chapter Eleven

We're Bolder, Not Older!

"A poet put it very well. She said when she was older,
She wouldn't be so meek and mild. She threatened to get bolder."

We're bold and we're beautiful! If you don't believe me, just dare me. I'll gladly hike up my skirt and head for the fun, and I know for sure I won't be alone.

Once the word got out that older and bolder was the way to be, I started hearing from all sorts of women with adventurous audacity. Some ride Harleys, others are touring the country in vintage cars, and we even have a Red Hatter who is the oldest woman ever to compete in the Winter Olympics. We call her Grandma Luge because she gets her jollies flying down mountains feet first.

Try these tips for making your pages as bold as your adventures:

 Be brave: Add beads that shimmer and shake and small props that can set a page on fire.

Congregate craziness: Gather an assortment of photos of brash Hatters behaving boldly and put them on the same page.

 Experiment with new techniques: Don't do the same old thing. Learn how to create three-dimensional images, or try snaps, eyelets, and brads on pages. Teach yourself a new skill for scrapbooking.

Walk on the wild side: Use your imagination and consider something crazy like a bra strap on a gift bag or wrap a gift with a glove.

I recently retired after 42 years of Teaching high school. I bought myself a Harley, and joined the Red Hatters. I'm having a blast as a Red Hatter. Traveling on my Harley!

Ruth Ann Hutchison

Happy Harley Hatter

This Red Hatter is convinced there is a Harley heaven. Stick-on letters combined with the rub-on transfer word "live" get the message across. Rub-on transfers are available in lots of fun fonts and are easy to use.

It's never too late  to

GET OUT and

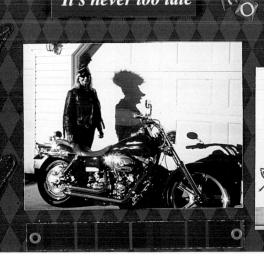

live

A poet put it very well. She said when she was older,
She wouldn't be so meek and mild. She threatened to get bolder.
She'd put a red hat on her head, and purple on her shoulder,
She'd make her life a warmer place, her golden years much golden.

We read that poem, all of us, and grasped what she is saying.
We do not need to sit and knit, although we all are graying.
We think about what we can do. Our plans we have been laying.
Instead of working all the time, we'll be out somewhere playing.

We take her colors to our hearts, and then we all go shopping
For purples clothes and hats of red, with giant brims a-flopping.
We're tired of working all the time, and staying home and mopping.
We order pies and chocolate fudge, and rich desserts with topping.

We crown ourselves as duchesses and countesses and queens.
We prove that playing dress-up isn't just for Halloween.
We drape ourselves in jewels, feathers, boas, and sateen.
We see ourselves on television and in magazines.

We laugh, we cry, we hug a lot. We keep each other strong.
When one of us goes out for fun, the rest all go along.
We gad about, we lunch and munch, in one big happy throng.
We've found the place where we fit in, the place we all belong.
"Ode to the Red Hat Society"
by Sue Ellen Cooper

Happy Red Hatting!

It's all Downhill

That's Grandma Luge above me in
the red hat. She said she was proud
of being the oldest woman to
compete in the Winter Olympics,
but wasn't quite prepared when
her age was announced to specta-
tors all over the world as she
entered the stadium during opening ceremonies.

Technique

Popping off the Page

Illustrations and graphic elements become bolder when they are multi dimensional and rise from the page. It's easy to create this effect. First, begin with three identical copies of the same image (A). Gift tags work well. Remove one side of the backing and place foam square on first image (B). Remove top backing and place another foam square on top of the second image and repeat the same procedure (C). Gently press the two images together (D). Repeat procedure with third image (E and F). You can add as many layers as you like. Bigger is bolder!

BORN to Be wild

Chances are good these Red Hatters have never met, but their antics landed them on my page of brash beauties. Rubber stamps are easy to use and a great way to customize labels to suit the photos on a page.

SHE WHO LAUGHS LASTS!

Ready to Race

Adding fanciful trims can add emotion to a page. The beaded trim can fly with the wind when the Harley honeys take off with a zoom.

We're just getting started!

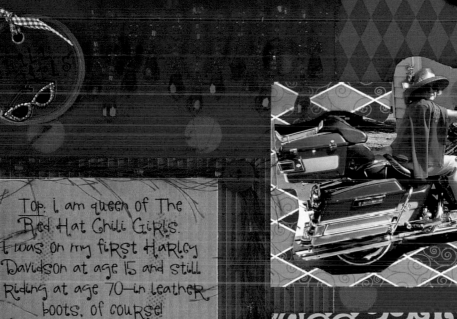

Top: I am queen of The Red Hat Chili Girls. I was on my first Harley Davidson at age 15 and still Riding at age 70—in leather boots, of course!

Below: Just having fun sitting on my neighbors Harley before going out to dinner.

Project

Glove Gift Wrap

*M*y mother always told me good things come in small packages. I used to think she said that just to make me feel better about being height challenged. I have learned over the years that she was right, and that the small box has everything to do with what's inside. Just like me!

Materials:

1 jeweled crown charm

1 polyester stretchable glove, red

1 surgical glove

7" lace trim, purple

Hot glue gun

Pipe cleaner

Stretchable bracelet, optional

This gloved hand (A) holds a surprise for a special Red Hat Society friend. To make, attach purple lace to trim cuff with hot glue gun. Glue crown charm to ring finger of glove. Put surgical glove on your hand (B). Gently put red glove on over surgical glove (C). Be sure surgical glove fits down into all fingers of red glove (D). Carefully remove both gloves without letting surgical glove pull out of any of fingers of red glove (E). Insert small gift box inside glove (F). Place stretchable bracelet on cuff of glove (G). Gather top of surgical glove and blow into it; inflate as if it were a balloon (H). Twist surgical glove shut and secure tightly with pipe cleaner.

Wrapped and Ready

If the joy is in the giving, I say make it even more joy-filled by wrapping a gift with reckless abandon. Simple paper gift bags can be decorated in countless ways. A bag can be in the same fashion as a scrapbook page (left), or you can add a sheer bag to the outside and do double duty (rear center). The back support leftover from the bra purse project reminds its recipient to hang loose and "Let it Go! (right). A gloved hand (front center) holds a special secret.

Just Let

Scarlett STRUTTERS

hattitude

We're just getting started!

friends

reducation

On Fire!

Here's a way to add a spark! Adding matches and tissue paper flames made all the difference in avoiding a conventional scrapbook page. Dip the tips of the matches in hot wax to make them safe from catching on fire.

The fire department gets this antique fire truck out for special occasions and having us ladies as passengers was certainly special. We got lots of laughs and honks from passerbys. After the fun of riding the truck, members enjoyed a day in the park with crafts, foods, antiques

diamond
32 COUNT
STRIKE ON BOX MATCHES
CLOSE BEFORE STRIKING. KEEP AWAY FROM CHILDREN.

CAMEL RIDES

WILLIAMSTON
FIRE DEPT
ENGINE
1936

It's never too late to have a happy childhood.

Chapter Twelve

Red Hatters Celebrate Mirthdays!

"We gad about, we lunch and munch, in one big happy throng."

I have long believed in the party system. I say find a reason to have one any chance you get! Red Hatters don't shy away from celebrating birthdays or any other good reason to congregate for merriment. I say bring it on!

Don't limit celebratory pages to marking the days of birth. Use any excuse you can to pass on a smile and cheer. I don't think we should just celebrate Mirthdays, we should create a few too, including;

Reduation: The passing of a pink princess into Red Hathood upon her 50th birthday.

Night on the town: You never know where you may end up or who may crash your party. Keep a camera handy; sometimes total strangers want to join your fun.

Wedded bliss: Celebrating marriage knows no age limits. More and more Red Hatters are finding their way to the altar with Red Hat Society attendants in full regalia. Record the moment in Technicolor.

Just because: Wherever Red Hatters gather with glee is reason for a Mirthday celebration. Gather often with gaiety and enjoy!

Big Mirthdays that celebrate age tend to end in a zero, so be sure to make a special page for such a landmark. The Exalted Queen Mother invited the throngs to help celebrate her 60th in New York City.

Sue Ellen and Carmen Fletcher from the Folsom Dam Dames of Folsom, Ca. and the Sacramento Delta Divas celebrated their birthdays on July 22, 2004 at The Birthday Bash in New York.

Cheers for a Cure

There is special meaning in the pink plumes on this Red Hatter's hat. She is part of a group celebrating their survival after battling cancer. Heart-warming stories deserve to be told, and can bring courage to other Red Hat sisters.

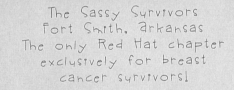

The Sassy Survivors
Fort Smith, Arkansas
The only Red Hat chapter exclusively for breast cancer survivors!

We hosted a book party featuring "Fun and Friendship after Fifty" at Waldenbooks on June 2, 2004. Queen Mother Jimmie Stokes served the cake provided by the book store. Approximately 60 Red Hatters from area chapters attended and many went home with a copy of the book. The feather on the cake was purple-but it could have been pink, as we wear pink plumes on our hats in celebration of being a "survivor."

Petite Purse

Sew a simple purple bag from felt and trim with red rickrack. The handle is made by stringing silk flowers on a piece of clear plastic tubing. Copy a color portrait of me onto iron-on transfer paper. Iron the image on a piece of muslin and cut me out. Dress me up however you like with feathers and jewels. Use a simple appliqué stitch on your sewing machine to sew the image to the bag.

Happy Red Hatting!

The Crimson Crones of Portland, Oregon celebrated their third birthday party in February 2004. Queen Jill surprised her ladies with a barbershop quartet.

The barbershop quartet serenaded the group with upbeat and sentimental songs while wearing red hats.

Celebrate One for Fun

Many chapters mark the anniversary of their first gathering with a Mirthday party. Your page can reflect the fun with whimsical details such as paper flowers. Trace and cut flowers from purple paper. Roll the petals loosely around a pencil to curl, then add a button at the center.

Merry Mirthday Card

A Mirthday card can be a keepsake to be enjoyed over and over if it is made with sturdy materials. The trick to this card is that it is made using iron-on scrapbooking fabric. Look for 12" x 12" fabric squares in scrap-book supply and craft stores. Iron fabric to the cardstock or paper. Here, a red cotton canvas fabric was ironed to purple paper. The canvas side is the exterior of the card. The fused fabric and paper is folded and scored so it closes like an envelope. Trim outside edges with metallic purple rickrack and seal shut with a costume jewelry pin. Decorate the inside with whatever sentiment and images you like.

All Set to Party

Red Hat friends often do a great deal of work to create the perfect setting for gatherings. Photos don't always have to include people; sometimes the tables and decorations tell a great story. Preserve the invitation and party favors on the page.

Welcome!!!

Mankato's Magnificent Red Hatters

Garden Party Brunch Menu
Scarlet O'Hatter
Paprika Egg & Ham Bake
Red Hatter Fruit Medley
Cinnamon Coffee Bread
Coffee & Tea

July 10, 2004

Mankato's Magnificent Red Hatters

tea time

Surprise Bridal Shower for Beryl Hutson at Lucils Tea Room

Shower with Happiness

Here comes Red Hat Society pride! When Red Hatters celebrate a happy day, it's never conventional. Hats and party horns announce the upcoming wedding of a Red Hat Society sister.

The Prim Roses
of Sugar Hill, Georgia

MUSEUM & HALL of FAME

Out for Frolics

Red Hatters are in a league of their own, and once in awhile they enjoy baseball too. A large baseball and bat commemorate a trip to the Baseball Hall of Fame. Simple shapes can be cut from paper and embellished with trims and ribbon.

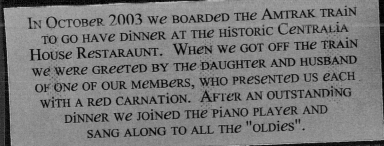

In October 2003 we boarded the Amtrak train to go have dinner at the historic Centralia House Restaraunt. When we got off the train we were greeted by the daughter and husband of one of our members, who presented us each with a red carnation. After an outstanding dinner we joined the piano player and sang along to all the "oldies".

Fresh-Picked Joy

Roses are red, Hatters are too. Look closely at photos and try to find something you can pull from the picture and use on the page. In this case it's red flowers. A simple white mat makes a big difference in the presentation and is well worth the extra minute it takes.

So much
more than purple and red.

The Red Hat Society is an international "disorganization" of women who embrace the worth of deepening friendships and re-discovering the value of play. Underneath the frivolity, we share a bond of affection and a genuine enthusiasm for wherever life takes us next.

To learn more about the Red Hat Society:
www.redhatsociety.com

To request membership information by mail, please send your name, address and phone number to Red Hat Society Information Requests, P.O. Box 768, Fullerton, CA 92836.

There's Only One...
Join The Fun!™

"A fond farewell from me and Frosty, the royal dog."

144